ADORABLE CORNER

Bold and Easy Coloring Book with Cute Creatures in Cozy Places

Cuddly Dragons serie

By Juno Giggles

We appreciate your support and hope you find joy in this book.

When you use this book...

It is advised to have
a sheet of paper behind the page you are coloring
to avoid any bleed-through that may occur.

Don't forget...

To leave us a honest review on Amazon.
It helps us get better.

Share your art and connect with us:
LIKE - SHARE - FOLLOW

SCAN ME

COLOR TESTING PAGE

LIBRARY

FISH SHOP
FRESH FISH

BAKERY

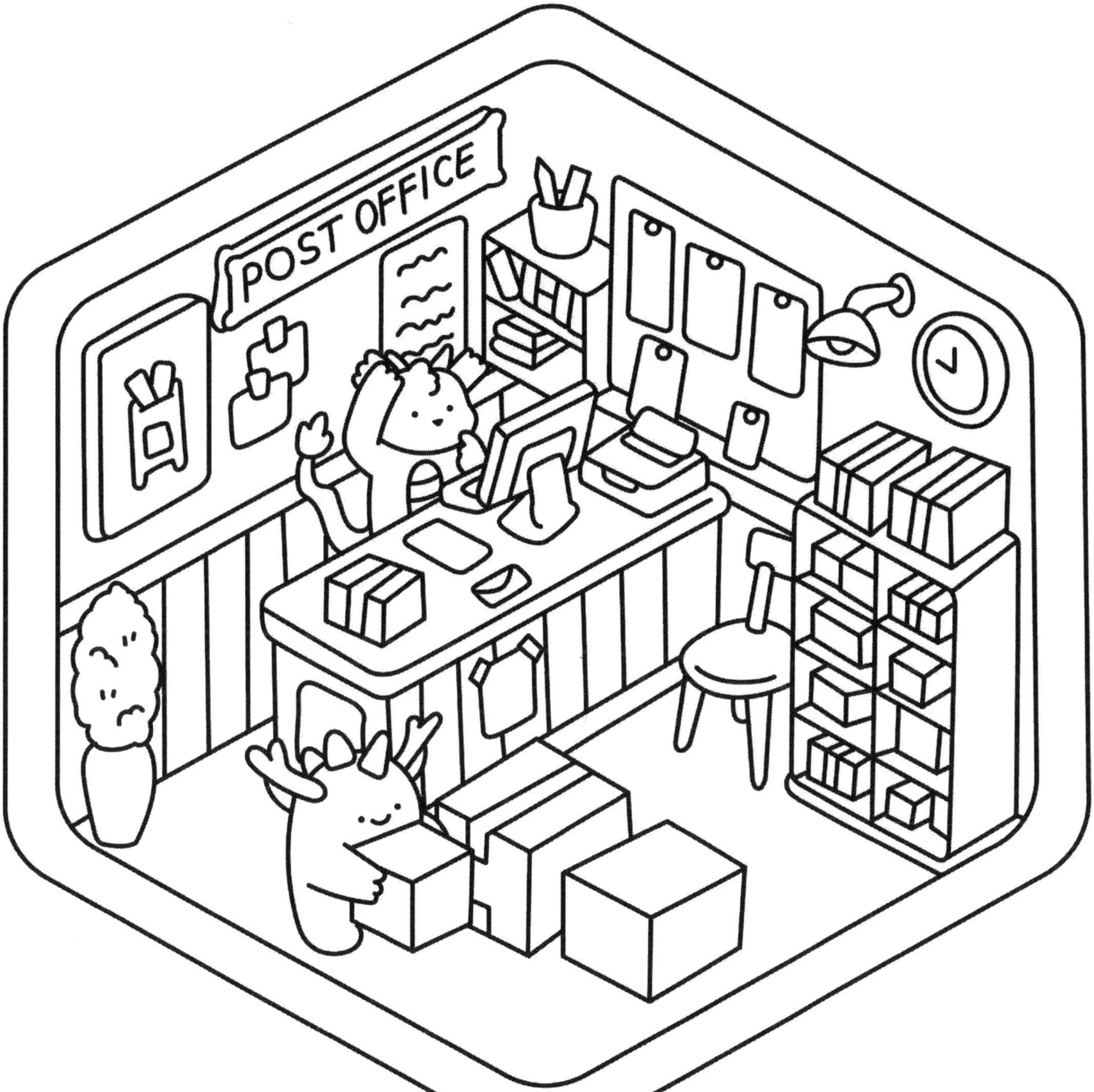
POST OFFICE

PIZZA
PIZZA

BIKE
SHOP

ICE CREAM
MENU

WELCOME

FRUIT & VEGETABLE
FRUIT

LIBRARY

SNACK SNACKS
POPCORN
NDY
NDY
POPCORN

Thank you for purchasing this book.
We hope you have as much fun coloring the pages as we had creating them.

If you loved this book, don't hesitate to **SHARE** your art or **REVIEW** this book. Feedback helps us improve and reach more coloring enthusiasts like you.

Visit us to learn more and get fresh coloring pages weekly!

SCAN ME

CUDDLY DRAGON SERIE

CONTACT: Info@junogiggles.com

Made in the USA
Las Vegas, NV
25 February 2025

18674041R10046